Written By Paul and Danielle Connor
Illustrated by: Leslie Haugen

We want to inspire kids to be creative and use their imagination!

ISBN 978-0-692-84121-1

The Christmas season was fast approaching and there was trouble at the North Pole! Santa began to worry about how he was going to keep track of so many children!

He called for an emergency meeting with his two senior elves,
Madi and Hudson, to see what ideas they had.
They realized they may need more help!

Santa decided to split the elves into two teams. Team 1 was the girl's team: Madi, Eliza, Erin, and Avery.

Team 2 was the boy's team: Hudson, Caleb, Emmitt and Simon.

Each team was given the same task of helping Santa keep track of all the children. The elves were so excited to come up with a plan to help make Santa's job easier!
Both teams ran off singing and jumping for joy.

It had been three long days and the elves couldn't wait to share their ideas!
Each team brought in what they had created wrapped with a big bow.
Santa said, "On the count of three each team will unwrap their invention.
1.......2........3!!!!!!"

Both teams shouted, "SANTA CAM!!!!!" Santa could not believe it!!!! Both teams had created the exact same thing. The elves were shocked as well. It looked like both teams knew exactly what Santa needed!

Hudson turned to Santa and declared,
"The Santa Cam will allow you to easily check-in to see when kids are being
kind to others, listening to their parents, and making good choices!"

Madi exclaimed, "And children all over the world will be able to tell you what they want for Christmas through this device!"
"Once they receive the camera they can place it anywhere in the house. The red light blinks to show that it is on!"

Santa was delighted to hear that his elves had come up with such a
great idea and that they all agreed on the same thing! He belted out,
"HoHoHo," and smiled from ear to ear!
He knew his job would be much easier this year!